Lost Boyz To Men

From My Heart To Your Eyez A Poetic Story of
Trauma, Transparency, and Triumph

Marquis Jackson

Printed in the United States of America

Visit www.iamredinspires.com for resources and booking opportunities.

Dedication

This book is foremost dedicated to myself. Writing this book over the last 20 years has been very therapeutic. These poems have helped me through my darkest moments in life, while at the same time giving me the most brightest hopes in life.

I also want to dedicate this book to any child that feels lost in life. I Aspire to INSPIRE all of you with the words of this book. Dark moments in life are just that, MOMENTS not forever. You will eventually be able to look within yourself and see the light shining through that the world is waiting to see. So please don't let bad moments turn into bad days.

I would also like to dedicate this book to my loving wife. I love you for awakening my greatness.

For the longest I never saw the greatness within myself, but with your persistence and loving encouragement I now see the man you've always seen. I now see myself as an unstoppable man and I appreciate you for helping me to become the best version of myself.

Lastly, to my beautiful children, thank you for being my joy. I love all 4 of y'all dearly, y'all are my WHY. Y'all are the reason why I strive to get 1% better everyday. And being a great father to y'all is not only a responsibility that I take seriously, it is also an honor. I promise to ALWAYS be there for y'all and I will NEVER let y'all down.

Foreword

My baby love. My gentle gangsta. My everything. I don't remember a time where I wasn't madly in love with you and your very nature and essence. Even more importantly, I have admired your brilliance and strength through my own personal camera lens of reality and I am fortunate to call you mine. I am honored to be able to share your beauty and awesomeness with the rest of the world. I am forever grateful for the time that we've spent thus far and for the fantastic family you've blessed me with.

You are a true wordsmith, poet and your authenticity and beauty transcends this universe. As you know, I was quite nervous when you asked me to construct your foreword. It wasn't that I did not want to do it nor was it that I did not have the words; in fact, I knew that I had too many! I cannot contain the excitement and relief that I felt when you decided to expose this very vulnerable side of yourself.

You have always been more than enough, more than capable and more than great. You are fully equipped for what is coming your way and I am blessed to have a front row seat to what is slated to be a beautiful expedition. I have always known that you were the very embodiment of greatness and royalty. Your illustriousness is boundless and the value that you bring to everyone around you is significant. I am elated that you are able to see and recognize that as well. You have always been ready for this journey and just like with all other trips, I have already packed your bags and can't wait to travel this gorgeous journey with you!

'Til the lights go out . . . xoxo

Preface

A lot, if not all my poetic work, stems from personal experience. They are stories of my truth and vantage point. Whether that be from my painful past, my wonderful present, or my magnificent hope for my future. My childhood consisted of many unfortunate events not uncommon to the stretch of road of which I grew up on. I began writing poetry at an early age as a constructive outlet. As a middle child, I rarely voiced my opinions, thoughts, or feelings verbally, so I leaked my unspoken words upon a piece of lined paper with the magic of a pen. As of today, I have a wonderful family which consists of my beautiful wife and four amazing kids. My family motivates me every day to never return to the life to which I once was accustomed, but rather to

soar to new and unrestricted heights which once presented itself as a mere fantasy. I have high hopes for my future and I look forward to growing old with my wife, watching my children grow up to be successful individuals with their own families, while never having to walk upon or even come close to my not-so-distant path. So, you are in for a wonderful yet intense treat. My collection of vivid artistry will not cease to amaze and enlighten the audience. As you embark upon this lyrical journey, allow your visual senses to take you through a small collection of my unyielding thoughts. Enjoy!

Introduction

Twenty years is more than a passage of time; it's a journey, a tapestry of moments woven with thoughts and emotions. Each day, each hour, I found words to capture fleeting feelings, to translate life's myriad experiences into verses. This book is the culmination of two decades of exploration, reflection, and introspection. It is not just ink on paper; it's a piece of my soul, a testament to my growth as both a human and a poet. Along this journey, I encountered joy, pain, love, loss, and the myriad nuances in between. I've tried to capture all of it within these pages. I invite you to embark on this literary journey with me. Within these pages, you'll not just read poems but feel the pulse of two decades of my life. May my verses resonate with your heart, as they have with mine. Thank you for allowing me the honor of sharing my soul's labor with you. This is a gift from my HEART to your Eyez.

Contents

"LOST BOYZ"

They say once you get institutionalized you mentally stop growing
but if you go through something so traumatic you can also stop
growing
I was 14 years old when my mom left me and went to rehab. That
was the day I stopped growing

That was the day that whatever feelings I once had, I stopped
showing I remember that night so vividly
I came home to my mom crying saying she needed help I could
tell she was tired of living in so much misery

It hurt me to my soul to see my mother cry like that

I knew she wanted to get the help she needed but leaving me in
the process to do that, oh nah I didn't like that
But I told myself it was for the best I was just glad she wanted to get
clean But I was still traumatized, I knew she needed to go but I
really didn't want her to
leave

And those hurtful emotions led me down a long dark path

It's like I was acting out doing everything I could to fuel my negative emotions which only led me to a emotional car crash

Overtime I learned to reason with myself and saw the good in the situation

So to see my mom's face lit up like a fixture was all I needed to see for me to stop misbehaving

However in this situation It took me years to grow from a boy to a man

I still had resentment of my mom for earlier choosing drugs over me and my sisters, so for years trying to reconcile wasn't in my plans

My wife always tried to encourage me to talk it out with my mother

But I always refused because in my stubborn head I had grew up without a mother so there was no need for us to talk it out with each other
Then one day my mom brought some heartbreaking news to me and my sisters

She told us she had cancer, at that moment that voice in my head telling me to talk to your mom about your feelings became a whisper

A whisper that was fading away like a dying breath

Emphasizing to me that my time was running short to have that talk with my mom that I know I needed I just needed right help

So eventually that conversation happened

It was a very emotional conversation but it had to happen

Due to the results During that last few months of her life because of that conversation, we had the best bond I could long for

And that's just one of my many life stories of me transitioning to a man from a Lost Boy

"LOST AND FOUND"

You ever wonder why we do what we do and why we say what we
say Because we only see the dark spots of life we aint exposed to
the day But today you gonna feel what I feel on that statement
Willie Lynch said 300 years, but we still live in slavery

We look different at each other, but real difference is from sides, to
shades, to ages it's so much confusion between that it causes
frustration
Brought up to believe the folks our same age know all of the
answers Listen and respect your elders, HUH?! in our eyes that's
dying like cancer They got us brainwashed this is owners mode
they know our every move So when we try to cut them puppet
strings them folks is on the move
And I aint talking bout the white folks, I'm talking black America
We let our life repeat itself, it's just like truth or dare to us
They the truth and we the dare, I guess that's why they scared of us
But that's all in their plan our mentality we don't give a WHAT!
It's like they know the truth and dare us to come and get the
knowledge They got us scared of change, so we use the streets to
get the knowledge But what they don't know is, the streets done
made us stronger than ever

Yea I know they think we dumb, but our hearts are strong, and our minds are very clever So its whatever, you tell me what you wanna talk about

My vocabulary is two times your so what you talkin bout You think because I'm from the streets, I can't think with the best

While you sleep I make a plan, when you rest, its full effect So think twice before you judge me, I am not the one

I am 2nd to you, but to me I am the only ONE I'm not amazing grace but I was blind to life But all I see now is success, so I shine to life

So I am only me, and I am the only one who knows where I been around Similar to amazing grace, was LOST but now I'm FOUND

"THIS WORLD GOT ME GOING CRAZY"

Sitting on my front porch getting real clouded Thinking of the
world's ways got my mind crowded I can't even make my own
decision
If I do something wrong, where is the right within it?

So I say forget it you tell me what's the business

I wanna know what you think about this life that I'm living Was
the young man born cursed just for the reason
Eve was tempted, tempted Adam for the fruit of their pleasing I
don't know the answer now, I'm on this life time search
I need to know just how I feel and what's the reason I hurt I heard
once you pass away you heading back to the dirt
Well please hurry bring your light because all this darkness is murk
My attire is all black from all the pain in my past
Dress me with a white casket, let me be when I pass This world got
me going crazy let this life be my last I'm searching for the
paradise where can I find it I ask?

"PRODUCT OF MY ENVIROMENT"

Late nights under the city lights, I heard gunshots and sirens all through the nights… I'm just a product of my environment

I learned never run from the "Red Dogs", because if they catch you, they'll beat and leave you left for dead dog…I'm just a product of my environment

Running around on the playground, it was normal to see used condoms and junkie needles when I looked down… I swear I'm just a product of my environment

A Dice game going good, almost always ends with someone getting their head bust in the hood… I'm just a product of my environment
Steal a car take it to the chop shop and strip it, my cousin taught me I could hustle anything and flip it… yep, I'm just a product of my environment

A drug fiend lighting up in the basement, got the whole downstairs stankin while she blazing… I'm just Living as a product of my environment

Riding with a whole pound of weed in the car, had me paranoid every time I saw a cop car… but that's expected because I'm just a product of my environment

Waking up in a cold house with no food forced me to rob, steal, and deal I had to do what I had to do, why… Because I'm a product of my environment

First child at 17 had to grow up, no one told me how hard it would be transitioning from a boy to a grown up… I'm a product of my environment

No one ever told me the 4 felonies at age 17 would soon make it hard for me to get a job to provide for my family… I'm a product of my environment

Going through all I went through growing up from a child

Made me into this wonderful man, great father, and loving husband you see today so it was all worthwhile… to be a "Product Of My Environment"

"NO DIRECTION OR CORRECTION"

NO DIRECTION or CORRECTION I'm just me, I'm sorry you
can't accept it before you know me
Get to know me before you judge me, and I'll get to know you
before I trust you That's fair right? See your assumption of me got
me like Beanie Sigel I can feel your hate
in the air right?

Should I care though? Nah I would rather just walk by you and
watch you stare though Can I just speak my mind, live my life, and
be a head to my family?

Or do I have to impress her, answer to him, as you tell me to run
ahead of my family?

Nope I'll never leave them we stand tall side by side

And face every obstacle head on like we playing chicken in a car
ride No directions for my words I'm just venting a lil bit
Childhood full of pain got me sippin a lil bit Years of mental
wounds got my mind slippin a lil bit
Growing up hearing gunshots and sirens every night got me
trippin a lil bit Seeing that man put his hands on her had me
thinking he must be pimpin a lil bit...

A little more time in these streets would've got me 25 to life

I lived by the code "Death before Dishonor", so I probably would've died for them stripes Not no more though, now I live for my kids and my wife
The Og's taught me always stand 10 toes down and never run from a fight Now I teach the Og's folks aint fighting no more so now it's time to think twice Wassup cuz? Chilling bruh, yeah, I speak the lingo
How are you doing sir? Fine and you? I guess I'm just bilingual
NO DIRECTION or CORRECTION

"BORN SINNER"

Yea I'm a born sinner but I graduated to born winner

I done struggled every day in a cold world now I'm really hoping
for a warm winter Speak my mind never choke, my grandma
taught me keep my peace when I'm provoked

Sell dreams never dope, KING had a dream that started from a
hope Sometimes the motivation starts right from a quote
Some get discouraged fade away just like the smoke Inherent
imperfection got me getting old Government corruption got me
getting broke
This life is all I know so why should I complain I'm scraping up
change I'm just tryna to maintain
I'm trying stay right in my lane we all struggle some different some
same thing That's why we gotta keep each other going you know
that still waters are deadly got to
keep each other flowing

Never hesitate to help my brother when in need Family is all I got
so Family is everything I need
That's why I surround myself with people on the same mission
You can learn from anybody you just gotta pay attention Never
been a know it all that's why close my mouth and listen

You wanted food for your thoughts well come and get you some nutrition

"MINORITY"

I remember long nights, shivering under a sheet with no heat
walking around the house with a candle with no lights

I used to go to my neighbor house just to take a hot shower and get
a hot meal

then head back to a dark cold house my mom was mentally absent
so I was lonely for real
I once asked my mom if she cared if I smoked weed

I was crying out for help so any kind of attention at the time from
my mom is something that i wanted but I didn't know how to ask
or explain that it was what I need

my pride wouldn't let me beg and plead

my life was a failure so a goal of success is something I could not
achieve I didn't have any motivation, school was no longer a
priority
in my head majority of my friends had perfect lives while my life
was terrible, my emotions punished me to the point of feeling
treated unfairly just like a minority

"THE PAIN BEHIND MY EYEZ"

You can often catch me starring with a blank face

no I'm not mugging or trying to intimidate anyone, they say a person's eyes are a window to their soul well in mines you can find a empty space

some can relate and see the pain behind my eyez

an encouraging word can lift me up momentarily but soon after that I'm back down in the dumps struggling to rise

some things I've seen with my eyes might leave you surprised

like leaving school Friday and not eating again till Monday at school when I arrived seeing loved ones die year after year right before my eyez
I didn't drop one tear as a boy but as a man I've cried many times I guess when I was younger I was a volcano waiting to erupt reaching out for attention at home which I wasn't getting so I went outside to disrupt I was a menace to society because I was a product of my environment
I aint show no love because I aint get no love it was so easy to be violent I don't regret my upbringing it molded me into the man I am today but the pain behind my eyez is still here I just try to hide it everyday

"PRISONER"

Prisoner of my thoughts, captive to the four walls of my inner being.

I want to escape the grip, but it seems impossible in this world. All I can do is mourn on the inside until I'm free.

I hate this sickness I wouldn't wish it on my worst enemies

and I pray to God that my kid's don't have to go through this torture.

Torture. That's exactly what I feel 80% of the time but I have to act fine for the sake of my family.

But what do I do for the sake of my sanity?

I wish I knew the answer then maybe I could fight back in this losing battle.

But I can't so I'm constantly bullied. Bullied by my interior, breaking down my exterior.

In a fight that I can't win with everything to lose.

I feel like giving up, giving up like I'm being kicked when I'm down.

That is exactly what my mind does, kicks me when I'm down, plays on my insecurities, makes me feel worthless.

I want to scream, I want to cry, I want to curse, I want to.... DIE.
No worries though I'll
be fine and LIVE to fight this lifetime battle another day

"FRENEMY"

Everyone has an agenda, a motive or a intention so be careful who
you befriend

They may start off genuine however their jealousy, envy and hate
may be exposed by the end keep your grass cut low so you can see
the snakes coming before they bite you
they smile in your face while giving high fives behind your back to
people who don't even like you

just because you're cool with someone doesn't mean that y'all are
friends

true friendships are built on a solid foundation because if you
build a castle on a sand foundation eventually it will be taken away
by the waves and the wind

people will come into your life for a reason

some come into your life for a lifetime while others come into
your life for a season

"THAT'S MY DOGS FASHO"

You see my furry partnas made me feel complete

because even though my heart was void of my mamas love they stood by my side everywhere I went we was like one they didn't even need a leash

I come home at night from a dark cold world to a darker and colder house my house wasn't a home it was just me and my dogs sleeping on a lonely couch
I just want y'all to understand my dogs got me through my scariest nights just imagine it... 13 years old no food no heat no lights with all those odds against a person it's hard to even put up a fight man's best friend, well I wasn't a man then but they was red's best friends

I always seemed to isolate myself I guess I was a introvert because for some strange reason outside of my dogs I wanted less friends

I mean I had friends but they never knew of my secret pain behind my closed door yea I put on a show

but you know who helped me through my daily pain? Yup you guessed it, that's my dogs fasho

"TRAP STAR"

Trap star… what's the first thing that comes to your mind when you hear those words?
Maybe a hustler, baller, or shot caller moving those pounds and birds

Growing up I never wanted to be a trap star but the way my cards was dealt I had to do what I had to do

But I didn't do it for the fame, the glory, or the women, I did it for one simple reason, me and my mama needed food

I was in survival mode literally, if I didn't run to those cars and make that hand to hand transaction me and my mama couldn't eat

I was out all night sometimes, so instead of a bed I had to rush to school and that is where I would sleep

Another day and the same routine

Come home from school, drop my book bag off, and kiss my mom.
HOMEWORK??
Nah at this point of my life that wasn't part of my routine

Then back to the trap I go, The dope boy I was Pushin P for was the same dope boy Pushin P to my mom

He knew she was my mom but in a sense he understood me and my situation, he knew I was young and desperate just to get some funds

Every night after my shift was over so to speak

He would pay me and I would quickly say can you take me to a fast food restaurant so I can get me and my mom something to eat?

And he would do it, like I said he understood my situation

And I ain't have no shame in my game about asking every night without a hesitation I would get the food, come home and say ma you hungry I got some food
She would take the food and say thank you baby and close the door then I would head to my room

In this life the ball was in my court and life gave me every reason to lose
But I was determined to win by any means necessary even though I felt like I didn't even have a choice to choose

Like I said I never wanted to be a trap star

I had a light beaming inside of me begging to get out so that I could let my light shine upon the world but my circumstances left me feeling like a…"TRAPPED" star

"I AINT MAD AT CHA"

My version of 2pac's "I aint mad at cha" The Old me talkin to The
New me...: now we was once two niggas of the same mind
quick to holla at a shawty wit the same line jumped off the porch
at 14 then you hit the streets never ran from confrontation always
stayed in beef
you could care less about the consequences of ya actions you had
that hood nigga swag but you was never flashy white tee fitted hat
wit some fresh ree's
bout to roll up a blunt time to call Steve

then we get high as we walked up and down the hood some lil bad
young niggas up to no good
ima take you back a lil farther wit our homie O we used to goto
CVS and steal the whole store duffle bag full of candy when we go
to school and sell out by 6th period we was the truth
what about our white homie Chris he was a nigga too robbin
niggas for they bikes then bring em to the crew
but we had to make sure we spray painted tho our way of killing
evidence we wasnt thinking tho
you remember B.R.P. we used to act a clown we hit a party 10
deep and tear it str8 down
now everybody banning us from any other parties but we still
showed up reppin tryna get it started

you say its all in the past and tell me how you changed Oh you a
Jehovah Witness now I hear ya talkin mayne and I cant even trip
cause im just laughing at cha
you trying hard to maintain then go head cause I Aint Mad At Cha

"BATTLE TESTED"

Every scar tells a battle story

Whether you won that battle or lost, all that matters is you endured to tell that story, so that in itself is worth the glory

And these scars are not only physical they can also be emotional

And sometimes because of those scars it can lead us to have numb feelings with ourselves and others, in other words unemotional

PTSD, most of us have and don't even know it

And for us who know it, we try to mask it so even though we could be going through turmoil emotionally others wouldn't know it because we rarely show it

But when we finally get the courage to open up and tell our story everyone listens Like the scars of a lion we still maintain our throne but we couldn't do that without our supporting cast and mines is my family and friends and that list is too numerous to mention But I haven't always had that help I used to feel all alone

That was my comfort zone but trying to feel better from isolation didn't work I had it all wrong I couldn't overcome this by myself I needed that help to come out of that hole
But what good is that help if I never even attempt that grab the rope Eventually though I begin to see the light and the benefit of coming out of the darkness
I have a family that's waiting and relying on me so I have no choice but to get out of my mood of being heartless

I can't be selfish and isolate myself that's not fair to the ones who love me

Me accepting their love is the only way for these scars to heal so that I can have a effective recovery

Like I said every scar tells a battle story and every loss learns a lesson And I learned from all my scars that I will always be battle tested

"KING OF THE JUNGLE"

Even though I consider myself a beast and a king in my jungle,
there's still no peace So, I decided to release my pain on this pad
with my magic pencil trying to score high in
life although trying not to cheat
I promised myself that defeat will never come near me my reign
won't cease So, then I proceeded to load up my poetic gun with
my untamed thoughts and shoot
deadly words that will leave you with shivers from your head to
your feet You see I know that one day soon, there will be light at
the end of all my struggles
And I also know that for me to make my ends meet I have to hustle
Some people want the best for me while others want me to fail so
they drop blocks in my path so I can stumble

But I'm very clever, I'm one step ahead of you so when you drop
them stumbling blocks, I catch them blocks and juggle them up I
never fumble

A lot of people got life backwards like Bees and Bumble

But me on the other hand I'm focused to win this game of life as
the M.V.P with a triple double

This world is constantly dropping bombs all on me so I can tumble
But I'm a Lion so I claim my throne as "KING OF THE
JUNGLE" "THEY SAID I WON'T MAKE IT"
Ok I'm trying stay focused, but I go through the motions

I have been through so much pain I can't even let out emotions
Numb to the fact that I grew up with a mother on crack
She didn't care so why should I school went straight to the back Of
my priorities, foot race to death I was on track
On a marathon to the prison system no looking back Thinking, of
suicide had me scared to be by myself Had a knife to my wrist just
a cry out for help
I saw my sisters leave one by one and left me alone No one to talk
to so I shut down and went in a zone
Cold hungry nights got me thinking I don't want to go home
Anger expressed because anger was all I was shown
Seeing my mother get beat by that man had me ready to kill Him
or anybody else my wrath that had to feel
Statistically age of 25 THEY SAID I WON'T MAKE IT Well, I'm
26 now so I guess that I made it

"SHOOT FIRST ANSWER QUESTIONS LATER"

walking down the street minding his business another young black
male is beat or killed with no witness
and because there's no witness there's no media airplay

and now his mom is standing there grieving with a blank stare face
we hear about Mike brown Trayvon Martin and many others
I know of some personally who have been brutalized and
victimized and I'm sure you know of plenty others

I've had my hands up before... gesturing don't shoot

while I'm being aimed at with shotguns assault rifles and pistols
too

Was all that called for? Was it necessary for someone who is
unarmed? unfortunately we live in a world full of injustice with
chance takers

the power is in the gun which gives the person with the gun a
sense of irrational power so even if they see your hands up and
hear you yelling "DON'T SHOOT" there's a chance they'll still
shoot first and answer questions later

"IMPERFECTIONS"

I'm running for my life, while the police are just shooting people
to get stripes I'm still fighting for my life, even though my
ancestors fought for my rights
Rights to what though? I guess my right to remain silent/ silent as I
watch you beat or shoot me to death So that i can forever remain
silenced

It's a sad story for the state of the world

things are going from bad to worse every day the world twirls

Is this system heading toward one big police state, as the
government continues to control our fate?

I think we all know the answer to that as the media abandons love
and only promotes hate Division will break a community down
from within
so no matter the race, background, or culture if you turn one slave
against the other to the slave owner it is a win

You can more time for petty crime than a rapist who has had
multiple victims and whoever told you that racism doesn't exist in
2016 is a mental victim

I'm just speaking my truth you don't have to agree with it

my truth is from my vantage point of the smokey mirrors in the world so my third eye is open and I can see clearly with it

Why is it that a doctor can get paid more than a teacher? I guess because they can save your life

But a teacher is just as important because some of the valuable lessons you learn from a teacher can also save your life

I'm just trying to do right but what is wrong is always present within me

but I know that all these issues we as humans face comes with the territory as a direct deceiving from Satan to Adam and Eve
IMPERFECTIONS...

"THEY LOVE US IN CHAINS"

They love us in chains but they hate us in gold, that's why they
stripped all our gold then they laid us in boats
They aint gonna teach you this in school it aint in books that they
wrote facts to enhance your knowledge and impart wisdom
through quotes

Most of the distractions we see are as simple as well thought out
hoax
that sometimes leads to tension and a racial division is what they
intend to promote 2017...not close to slavery not far from the L.A.
riots and a racial civil war is still being provoked we see bad news
everywhere, from a swipe of a finger to the click of a remote/
people have been
wanting true peace and security but looking to governments to
provide that is to no hope

"FALLEN TEAR'

1,2,3 & to the 4/
another black man is killed by a police officers knee on his throat

This kinda stuff happens so often it's sickening
Trying to show love in a hate filled world is like trying to water a
dying plant with a water hose that's trickling

If I feel this pissed off about these situations I know God has to be
furious
He said and I quote "vengeance is mines" but when will he act to
take care of all this mess, I mean I'm just curious

I wasn't planning on watching the video because I knew the affects
it would have on me emotionally
I guess curiosity killed the cat because I watched it, and to see that
officer with his knee ever so casually on the guys neck with his
hands in his pockets I mean he looked like this was something he
did socially

And some wonder why cities are getting burned down
People are pissed, because peaceful protesting, marching, jogging,
etc. is going unnoticed so a burning city to have a voice heard is
something they earned now

2020...has been one heck of a year
To bad we're only half way through the year and we don't know
what the 2nd half will bring other than another fallen tear

"THOUGHTS TO MYSELF"

What is THIS, what am I SEEING, what am I LIVING, what about BELIEVING?

THIS is a crooked wicked and Twisted system.

I have SEEN Injustice everywhere I look. I'm LIVING my life walking on eggshells trying not to be another statistic

. I am BELIEVING that one day things will get better, and my faith in Jehovah fortifies my belief

. But in the meantime, I'm going to continue to teach my children, I will lead by example, I will remain neutral, I will remain positive, and I will remain loyal... thoughts to myself

"SHE TAUGHT ME HOW TO LOVE"

Never cried as a child but many times as a man what can I say, I am who I am

As a child I was wild, and plenty times as a man, again what can I say I am who I am I bottled up all those tears, growing up I never let them burst forth
Little did I know because of all those bottled up emotions I was dying on the inside I was equivalent to a walking corpse

I thought I didn't have anyone to talk to so I expressed my emotions in other ways Like acting out as a thief in the night or a robber in broad day
By the time I met my wife to be I was a emotional wreck

But she accepted me for who I was with warm hugs and tender kisses upon my neck She taught me to be vulnerable so I opened up to her
Little did I know that she would open up my floodgates of tears to flow right through her She never judged me she just listened compassionately
She helped me to realize that even though my emotions may be all over the place it was ok, she even helped me to think rationally

And for that I am and will always be thankful

When I look at life as black hole she would help me to see life
from a different angle So now instead of looking at the glass half
empty I see it as half full
She taught me how to love me, and now I can love her with
everything I have overflowing with a glass full

"TRUE BEAUTY"

Your true beauty is your brilliance not your pretty brown skin
complexion Not your pretty hair, sexy eyes, and lips, your
appearance is God's perfection
But I'm talking about your book knowledge, your street smarts, I'm
talking about your intelligence

I knew your mind before I knew your face, so your appearance to
me is irrelevant You want to know my real turn on with you?
It's not your sexy breast, thick thighs, or pretty feet that made me
get you

I saw a young lady in school grinding trying get it, making a better
way for a better future

Your late nights up studying, your early days teaching me about
the Truth, made me one to be a priority in your future

So, what is your beauty? Your physical appearance or your mental
intelligence?

I chose you for your True Beauty, the total package, your
appearance and your oh so sexy brilliance

Your drive to make something out of nothing is amazing to me

Grades got low, times got hard, but you stayed strong, that's also
amazing to me
You finish what you start, and get the job done right

It's been 7 years since we started growing, and the finish is to bring
in new life So now I'm telling you how much I adore and admire
your smarts
And now you know how much I Love You for your intelligence
and your beauty from the start

"EVERLASTING"

I still feel da same way I did about u when you stood by me in the
dark you led my way to the light

I made you a promise from the start that I would never walk out ya
life Now here we are almost two years later standing face to face
your eyes on my heart my eyes on your soul as we become one to
close the space At first I couldn't see this day with us not saying I'm
surprised
over the phone I grew to love for who you are not what you are on
the outside I appreciate that you accepted me regardless of all my
flaws
you always made my heart happy and the love I have for you will
never pause so, before we say "I DO" let's remind ourselves that
love is everlasting
now let's put our hearts and souls together and become what's
everlasting ONE LOVE THAT'S EVERLASTING

"A THREE-FOLD CORD"

A Three-fold cord is one that cannot be quickly torn

A new personality is something that cannot be quickly worn

But with Jehovah's help even the most challenging obstacle can be won

Marriage... A perfect union with 2 imperfect people with a strong bond

One day at a time is all it takes, Jehovah said rejoice with the wife of your youth...simply put enjoy your time together, and have fun

Hold her hand, verbally express your love for her and that's something she will always appreciate

Build him up, support him, and your value will never depreciate
Study together, preach together and most importantly pray together
Doing things Jehovah's way guarantees yall happiness and your family's longevity to stay together

Never allow a wedge for Satan to pry open into your lives

Because all he needs is a slight opening to infiltrate your happiness
with negative energy and bad vibes

When times get hard meditate on what Jehovah has brought yall
through as a family And never doubt Jehovah because to your faith
that can be damaging
Always rely on Jehovah, and never be quick to leave Because with
Jehovah's help your marriage will succeed

"RUNNING FOR NOTHING"

Have you ever woke up one day and felt like the drama from
yesterday woke up with you?

I have on plenty occasions, so I try to run from the situation but
then I think to myself" where will that get you?"

so I ponder on my question and I back flash on all the scenes I ran
from the confrontation I realize if I keep running for nothing I'm
basically running from Satan
or should I say for Satan? because isn't that simply what he wants
us to do?
run from what he brings into love, which is simply the word
HATE, why can't we do what GOD wants us to do?

speak mild words to turn away the rage, love one another at all
times, accept the things you can't change

I can't change the events that happened yesterday, therefore I'm
yearning for something

but today is a new day also the start of a new chapter if I aint
running for your love then I might as well be running for nothing

"FIGHTING FOR LOVE

I swear that you are special something more than just cordial Let
me open your mind and read you like Barnes and Noble
I'm here to wine you and dine you. Can I please take your order?

Give you the most and the best nothing less and no shorter And
I'm here to. compliment you

Never to hate you, or fail you, or contradict you

And girl don't worry about haters that's trying to dismiss you I see
your face and you light up just like some fixtures These last 10
years have been Kodak memory pictures
And I'm not worried about these other women with no credentials
With your potential no one else meets the standards
I want you all to myself a bed and a camera Give you the key to my
heart just never lose it
I loved you right from the start just don't confuse it With puppy
love that's for children yeah it's amusing Fighting for love but your
heart I will never abuse it

"I THINK HE'S LOSING HOPE TO SURVIVE"

It's getting hard out here, he's tryna to make his ends meet He has
bills with no money, he's just tryna to help his kids eat
However, he feels like he's stuck between a rock and a hard place

You want a dose of his life?? Just close your eyes and visualize and
come get a taste He thinks the government is lying to him, his kids
said "Daddy Why Us"
But he didn't have an answer, his thoughts were blown just like dry
dust I know you understand just what he's going through
So what he gotta do is what he gonna do

Negative thoughts are tempting but this man must be trippin
Because if he hit the Streets, he's sure to come up missing 10 years
of Probation and 5 more years to go
He's so far on the bottom, I think he's losing hope Once again...I
think he's losing hope
See this young man is lost therefore he doesn't know which way to
go He once heard people say "it's time for a change but he doesn't
really know
I feel his pain and I know you do too because people really broke

But it's O.K. he will bounce back a guarantee fasho

That little voice in his head you call a conscience told him "It's time to hustle up and do just what you know"

Then he said "If they won't give me a job I will create a job to feed my family, this life is all I know"

It's cold in this wicked world so he's gone grab a coat All the way at the bottom look up and see the hope He's getting gas with a pocket full of change
They say it's time for change but to him his life still seems the same He sees the same things that was happening 8 years ago and even worse
He went from playing in the clouds to laying in the hearse That's from the Top to the Bottom his life can't get much worse
He decided to give his wife and kids his Blood, Sweat, and Tears just to try to make it work

I am painting a perfect picture that his life aint picture perfect He runs his own business but he's wondering if it's working
He feels like Tupac when he said "ITS ME AGAINST THE WORLD"

And that's not his only issue lack of money is also causing problems between him and his girl

But whenever he fell on the ground he just Bounced back

You think he's gonna stay on the Ground? He has a family to take care of, so I doubt that
But it will not be easy for him because he has 4 felonies that make it hard for him to get work

But he also knows that it is not hard for him to go back to the streets and get work It's so hard to do right when he doesn't have a stable home
It's so hard to do right when all he know is doing wrong The unemployment rate is rising, and his bills keep on climbing
He's stressed out he can't even sleep because all his debt keep piling But he knows he can't give up right now his family is leaning on him
He made up his mind to give his last to his wife and kids even though the system is scheming on him

He is tired of this world he's sick and tired of being sick and tired
Therefore, he leans on his faith in God got to endure because God can never lie
God said faith without works are dead, so he's determined to gone stay alive From the bottom to the top, it's a guarantee that he going to SURVIVE

"YOU ARE APPRECIATED"

As I token of my appreciation, I thank you for everything you do,
you are appreciated For all the days you pushed forward even
when your days were blue, you are appreciated I thank Jehovah
every day for blessing me with you, you are appreciated
And without you in my life I swear I wouldn't know what to do,
you are appreciated I'm sorry for not telling you more that I
appreciate you but this is a start, you are appreciated
I vowed to you 14 years ago that you had my heart from the start,
you are appreciated Thank you for all the hard work you do for our
family, you are appreciated
You tenderly care for all of our needs and wants so for me not to
return the favor to you would be damaging, you are appreciated
Thank you for believing in my dreams and most importantly
believing in me, you are appreciated Thank you for seeing the
greatness in me even when I was too blind to see, you are
appreciated
Thank you for being a great mother to our children even when
you feel like you're not, you are appreciated

Thank you for always keeping yourself-looking good from your
head to your feet, you're more than a trophy piece you're my
everything and trading you in for anything else I would not, you
are appreciated

Thank you for holding me when I was down while at the same time motivating me to get back up/ you are appreciated

Thank you for seeing my vision and making it OUR vision now let's run these racks up/ you are appreciated

Thank you for loving me and for that reason I love you, I adore you, I honor you... BRANDY you are appreciated

"JUST A LITTLE WHILE LONGER"

A son, a grandson, a nephew, a cousin Gone to soon when we wish
that he wasn't
Oh how we all looked forward to seeing his first smile & hearing
his first laugh Watching his first steps and granny and pa pa giving
him his first bath
He would've been born into a family that gives unconditional love

and he would've got gifts year round not just on Christmas and on
his birthday but just because

we wanted to see him grow into a intelligent responsible black
man a man who would make his mother Jessica and father
Emanuel proud

but all hope for us to see these things are not lost all we have to do
is just wait a little while Jehovah God has given us hope a hope to
see our dead loved ones again
and at that time EJ will live forever without dying again
So even though we have a loss now in the near future we will win

so even though EJ has to rest in peace now/ in paradise he will
awaken from his rest to live forever not just a little while

"THE SON I ALWAYS WANTED"

When you was younger I would look at you and think to myself "I couldn't deny you even if I wanted too"

And even though you came into my life when I was still a child having a abortion is something I just wasn't gonna do

Watching you grow from a baby to a young man has been a privilege to say the least

Like how to be comfortable with being myself at all times and that's a lesson I learned from you that you can thoroughly teach

Even though you looked like me that wasn't enough

I wanted you to be like me you know, love sports, video games and be tough

But that's not, and now I come to appreciate that

See you have gifts, talents, and skills that I wish I had but I don't and that's a fact

So even though you may look up to me, in a lot of ways I look up
to you

And I know you feel like I'm lecturing at times but I'm just talking
to you like my dad and granddad talked to me, in the long run it
helped me and I know the wisdom will help you too

Be the 1st male Jackson in our family tree to graduate high school

You are smart, you got the brains to do it even though you don't
like school

Please be aware of your surroundings at all times, you're still a
black man in a racist world

And one day you will face some sort of racial injustice just handle
it cautiously and keep it moving like your forearm doing sets of
curls

I do hope one day you do decide to serve Jehovah on your own

But only you can make that decision so dedicating yourself to
Jehovah is something you will have to do alone

Always remember the principles I teach you to live by

I only want the best for you so learn from my mistakes and my guidance and a successful life for you will continue to arrive

A jr. you are not but you are my firstborn and only son and being a father is something I always wanted

And even though you are becoming your own man there's nothing I could do to change that and I won't try because to be completely honest you are and will always be "The Son I Always Wanted"

"LOVE IS"

I hope I set the right standards for you

I could never teach you how to be a woman but I can show you how a man is supposed to adore you

You are my 1st daughter my 1st princess soon to be a wonderful queen

Please... Always keep Jehovah 1st in your life and never let anyone or anything come in between

You are so smart you're so funny, your personality is attractive like a magnet

I just want to see you be the best you living your best life because I know your progress in life will never become stagnant

I'm sorry for the times I failed you as a father

Times when you need affirmation, a hug, or a simple smile, times like that when I was absent and I promise I will try harder

I will try harder until the day I die

Because being a father to you doesn't stop once your reach adulthood, I make a vow to you to be a father to you for the rest of my life

I want you to use your brilliant mind to make wise decisions in life and never follow your heart

Because even though your heart can play with your emotions its intent was to deceive you from the start

Be a leader that I have taught you to be

Who cares about the popular course in life, be a trendsetter and make your own course in life and walk it for as far as you can see

Mean what you say and say what you mean, always hold your head up and speak with confidence when you open your mouth

Love and respect yourself 1st and others will have to follow suit without a doubt/ Love is a part of your name for a reason

So everywhere you go in life let that love shine through you in every situation and fight for what you love for every reason

Kennedi Love... I Love You

"YOU ARE MY HART"

You have always and will always be my little firecracker you have the heart of a giant and you aint scared of anything that comes after you

Well, anything except a bug, but that's a small thing to a giant so continue to be a strong willed leader and many people will follow after you

But always remember being a leader comes with great responsibility

You have to lead people down the right path, and by your example you set along with your determination shows your versatility

I would never try taming your personality and don't you let anyone do it either

You are who you are so speak your mind respectfully and do so courageously as Jesus disciple Peter

I love you with all my heart and my goal for you is to be happy and successful

Whenever you have to stand up for yourself do so courageously but also respectful

and since we are talking about respect always treat yourself with respect

never lower your standards for anyone and always surround yourself around people who for your wellbeing is willing to invest

Never fight with your siblings and always have each others back

Always represent your family name well and never tolerate disrespect

Even though you can be tough you are still sweet as pie

And when things get rough you are the apple of my eye

In other words, I cherish you and my love for you is inseparable

So, for me not to love you with everything I have to give is unethical

My lil firecracker I love you with all my heart

I always knew you would have the heart of a giant so may your love for family, friends, and Jehovah never depart

"MY ROSE TO YOU"

You are pretty as a bouquet of roses

Your smile melts my heart like the sun when its frozen

You are only a baby now, so it's hard to tell what kinda lady you
will become

But my plan is to treat you like your sisters: princesses and some
queens to become

I can already tell you are gonna be bossy like your mama

And you are gonna have me wrapped around your finger just like
all the other young women in this house including your mama

It can be challenging at times tryna balance my love but I'm up for
the challenge

You are my last seed and carrying my last name with pride is
worthwhile and I know you can handle it

You've always liked to sleep on my chest I guess my heartbeat was
soothing to you

And I just wanna let you know you will always have my heartbeat to lay on if things get frustrating or confusing to you

You are my rose but not a dozen its ok to be different

And when you feel down like a fallen petal, I'll always pick you back up because seeing you happy is my everyday mission

Just like every rose has a thorn to protect itself

You too have a protection not only from me but most importantly Jehovah is always there for you when you need help

"OUR MIRACLE BABY"

So, I get the news you're pregnant ... What a wonderful day to me
how unfortunate we had to get the news after a car accident that
was a scary day for me congratulations the doctor said to us as we
looked at each other in confusion
you're pregnant he said and I'm like either he's trippin or I'm so
much distress that I'm having a illusion

little did I know that this pregnancy would be the most scariest
months of my life

my wife was soon put on bed rest there was a high chance that we
could've lost the baby's life just the thought of it now took me back
to a mental space that just wasn't right
my biggest fear next to losing my baby was having to choose to save
one either my baby or my wife

and I didn't wanna face that fear so I made sure I tried to do
everything right taking time off from work to make sure she didn't
want for nothing
Anything I could do to help, whether it was cooking grits in the
morning, driving to appointments in the afternoon while getting
the kids from school to cooking in the evening then getting the
kids ready for bed... I swear it was always something

but I wouldn't trade the experience I went through/

it taught me to appreciate you even more for everything you
contribute to me and our kids lives by everything that you say and
do

it is true that this was the scariest moments of my life

and there was many times that I prayed to Jehovah in despair many
nights I know how much you wanted me to give you a boy of your
own
but I know all we really hoped for was a healthy baby and every
time we saw that ultrasound I knew we wasn't alone

the doctors always had good news to say so I knew that Jehovah
had us covered

as we counted the months down to days and hours to minutes and
seconds then comes no other no other than Harli Rose Our
Miracle Baby

"SHOOTING STAR"

Don't follow my past learn from my present Don't do as I say if you can't learn from my presence
Once I was young and blinded to the facts of life

Now that I'm older I see clearly that my family are my plaques to life That's why I strive to be a true leader as the head of my family Because if I don't lead by example everything I do and say to my family can be damaging

So, to my children look at my past learn from my present and make application to your future

That way instead of being a falling star RISE to the occasion & make your star a shooter

"MY VILLAGE"

A village can only be as strong as it's chief and a chief can only be
as strong as his village

I know i am the chief of my village and that comes with great
responsibility and I'm grateful for the privilege

I have to make sure my village is well prepared and ready to take
on this wicked world

a world that is full of chaos and hatred and it's getting worse day by
day especially since Satan has been hurled

I can't afford to let my village be divided/ because division brings
about destruction that's why I strive to keep my village united

every village has issues but to every issue there is a solution

but there is only a solution if the matter is settled quickly because
procrastination can only lead to a toxic outcome of pollution

I plan on being strong for my village in any situation I will be their
shield in the face of any confrontation
my village will keep me balanced in everything I do say and think

my village is the heart of my eye, so I'll never take my eyes off
them not even to blink

"DEAR CANCER"

Dear cancer you took my mama and I hate you for it

I sat and watched her in pain wishing I had the power to replace it
for her I watched her struggle to breath it almost broke me down
I'm lying it broke me down all the way to the ground I see her
dying face when I lay down and close my eyes
and then them tears start forming and flowing from my eyes I
swear to God I hate ya...
I only got one mama I can't replace her you took her from me!

Man I miss those text messages she would send me my mama love
was so genuine it was more than friendly
Just the beginning, how long will this grief you caused me last?
kodak pictures got me thinking and re-living the past happened so
fast I wasn't prepared to see her struggle
wasn't prepared to go on living without a mother days full of
sadness, hoping for better days a struggle
the strongest woman I knew her heart was her biggest muscle

"DEAR MAMA"

Dear mama, I will forever miss you
I can't wait to see you again in paradise, I often picture the scene
of me running towards you to hug you and kiss you

You was a great mom I don't care what nobody else says

I always wanted to be around you, since I was a toddler you had
me hooked and I can't even remember that far back but that's what
everyone else says

I don't get sad as much as I used to when I think about you

And I know it's because my faith in Jehovah's promises has
fortified me so when I get down, he comforts me and gets rid of all
the doubt too

You remember talking on the phone for hours about movies we've
watched?

You would always tell the whole story even after I told you I ain't
seen it yet so don't ruin it for me and you would continue to just
run your mouth nonstop

I loved seeing you spend time with all your grandkids

The joy on your face brought joy to my heart that's why despite our earlier struggles I was determined never to keep you away from your grandkids

Lilah prays about your every night before bed

She really misses you and she can't wait to welcome you back in paradise, "please help me to make it to paradise so I can see grandma tee" is the exact words she says

You always had my back and best believe I always got yours too

Nothing can come between the love of a mother and her son, so if you got my heart ima take care of yours too

You have and forever will be the strongest woman I've ever known

I watched you overcome trials that would break the strongest person down but you endured effortlessly so defeat is something you have never known

Dear mama… I wish you was still here mama

"I LOVE YOU DADDY"

You are the best dad I can ever ask for I remember sitting on your shoulders as a toddler and looking up at the stars at night

You always guided me through life helping see how to view things that are wrong and right

You always taught me to be a level headed individual

And you always made our house feel like a home that was built with love, it was calm and livable

You greatest quality that I love about you is your patience

You always held it together with me and my sister even when we was testing your patience I'm sure your emotions were all over the place and racing

I loved when you would cook those big dinners and let me help

You taught me how to be sufficient as a man and help myself first before I'm able to give someone else help

I remember getting choked up the day that I moved out to move in with my wife And you comforted me with the short words "everything is gonna be alright"
I remember the day I got married you looked so proud

You raised me from a boy to a man and for that I just wanna yell so loud the beautiful words..."I Love You Daddy"

"MY GRANDS"

I have some great grandparents, their love never fails

Never failed to wrap me up when I used to get in my deep dark shell I can remember my Grammy would always know when I'm down
She would look in my room and say MARCUS! Come on up out this darkness and stretch them long legs, go walk around

Then I would take a deep breath and get on up
She would meet me at the door with a big ole hug which would always cheer me up She was the sweetest woman I've ever known She had so much respect and love in the community yet the only response I would see from her was her heart, humility was always shown

With my Grammy she was every one of my friends Grammy she loved all my friends like they was her own flesh

And forget Sunday dinners, every day was a Sunday dinner with some kinda meat, homemade biscuits, and some vegetables that was always fresh

And speaking of vegetables that was always fresh, my granddaddy had a garden that would put your favorite gardener's garden to the test

Now my granddaddy was the hardest working man I've ever known

His work ethic was unmatched and no complaints just a huge reason WHY he did what he did which was to provide for the family he's always known

He was a man a few words, but his presence was always felt

And when he would see his grandkids running around, he never would admit it but I know his heart would always melt

But don't get it twisted if it was smoke you wanted as a grandkid, he would be quick to grab a belt

Marquis gone ova yonder and grab me a switch because I can't find my belt

So, you think I'm bout to get a switch just so you can tear my behind up? Nah ima just run to my Grammy for help

And she would always have my back

JAMES! Leave the boy alone! Then she would tell me to get it
together and wouldn't fight back

Let me take you to the eastside with my other grandma and
granddaddy Jackie
One thing about Jackie he could definitely talk, I'm saying it
wasn't no two-way conversation with Jackie

When I was younger, I use to feel like he was always tryna preach
to me But not with no scriptures more so with life lessons
Lessons he learned the hard way growing up in the era he did, the
stuff he would tell me about his near-death experiences had me
thinking for him to be here still alive is nothing short of a blessing

As I got older though I learned to appreciate those conversations

I saw the wisdom he had and to listen to it as a adult helped me
through a lot of situations Now grandma she was and forever will
always be my rock
She would stop anything to come to my aid, literally life and death
instances and she was always there to help the tears stop

I hated that I disappointed her by dropping out of school/

But she never judged me she just told me "You will get through
this and I will help you through it too"

Everyone always says I was grandmas favorite and I think so too
But that ain't up for me to decide I'll let her tell you
Her home was also a safe place for many

Her love wasn't limited it was limitless, so she had enough love to
feed plenty I look forward to her not having to deal with all the
health issues anymore
Because in paradise Jehovah will make her vigor stronger than ever
then she can get back to doing what she loves and plenty more

Speaking of things she loves I remember going fishing with her
and Jackie all the time when I was a kid

But honestly if the fish wasn't biting and it was hot I was soon be
ready to go a lil bit
But every time I would have to wait for hours before that time
came

And I tell you what, I learned patience fasho because until she was
ready to go I would just have to chill until that time came

Overall I had the best grandparents anyone could wish for

And I promise to uphold their legacy and seeing all of them in
perfect health is something I always pray and wish for

"PURPOSE"

To all you mothers, God put life into you on purpose

You were called to be great, you were called to answer with
purpose Never feel like your efforts in life wasn't worth it
Because whenever you are tired from life beating you down, God
is busy working God was busy working to let you know your life
isn't worthless
My grandma taught me to just do your best and let God do the rest

And I just wanna relay the same message to y'all, do all you can
and God will do what you can't

Rest in peace to my mother I wish she was still here

but I honor her by honoring y'all so the love I have for her is still
near Near to my heart like handkerchief on a nice suit
In life you only get 1 mother and mines was great but when I look
at y'all in the crowd I see other mothers that are great too

I aspire to INSPIRE each and every one of you to NEVER give up,
your life is not worthless

Like I said God put life into you on PURPOSE, so as you leave this event today make up in your mind and heart that no matter what life throws at you...You will live your life with PURPOSE

"GENERATION CURSE VS. GENERATIONAL BLESSING"

Financial literacy...who's responsibility is it to teach it?

The schools won't teach it, and kids only listen to their friends so if the parents teach it will their kids even believe it?

How can kids set goals with no intent to achieve it

How can they build a mindset of generational wealth if their minds have not first received it If you answered they can't, you are absolutely right
That's why as parents and mentors it's not only our responsibility to teach our kids financial literacy it is also our God-Given right

We want our kids to leave the nest and not fall but take flight

We don't want our kids to start learning how to be financially responsible after they leave home, because if they do they will be behind the 8 ball in life and that is a battle no one wants to fight

That was my exact life experience slash lesson

Not learning how to pay bills until it's time to pay bills, not knowing how to save until I wished I had saved, not knowing cash is not king but credit is etc. etc. it was more like a generational curse instead of a blessing

But like a said that was my lesson

therefore I learned from it so now to my kids I can impart knowledge, understanding, and wisdom to break the generational curse and to become a generational blessing

I had to put my team on my back and carry em to the finish line Because when one of us win we all win, so I won't stop until I'm finished trying Trying to become more knowledgeable so that I can impact generations to come
And That generation starts with my kids, so instead of being cursed and poverty-stricken they will be blessed, and financially literate is what they will become

"POTENTIAL TO BE GREAT"

I have the potential to be great, but inconsistency won't let me

I start something never finish it, I guess persistency left me

Left me where I started right in the beginning

It's like starting to race, taking a early lead and eventually quitting
even though I'm winning

Sounds crazy huh? I can't figure it out either

It's like I tell somebody a idea that I'm pursuing and they like yea
that's a good idea, and they don't even believe it

So, this time around ima keep my thoughts to myself

Less talk More action time to level up to another step

I will learn to be consistent in all areas of my life

And if I don't do it for nobody else ima be GREAT for myself, my
kids, and my wife

"CONSISTENCY BATTERY"

Sometimes the biggest consistent parts in life is being inconsistent

It's like you start off doing everything right, but what you lack is
consistency
I've been that way with plenty of my goals That's why it's so hard to
achieve those goals I start off going hard with laser sharp focus
I might even have a measure of success then gradually I start to fall
off and lose focus 100 days of consistency can all be torn apart by 1
day of inconsistency
And that momentum you once had is now gone so being
consistent now becomes a deficiency But not all is lost, I just had
to get my priorities back in line
One day turns to two, 2 days turn to 4, four days turn into a week.
what I'm trying to say is I just had to take it one day at a time

Then before I knew it I was back to my focus

So if you fall down get back up shake the dust off and tell yourself
your situation is still worth trying it's not at all hopeless

I was taught, repetition+consistency=Mastery

So whenever that inconsistent bug bites you and drains you out, kill that bug by regrouping and recharging your consistency battery

"SATISFY ME"

Chasing money will never satisfy me

I realized that this year when I sat back and thought about all of my ideas I pursued that didn't even gratify me

I knew I had to make a change but what would I do?

Well instead of chasing money, chasing my dreams is what I should do I learned, an abundance of money doesn't bring true lasting happiness

Money doesn't give me the happiness I would feel if I was the heavyweight champion But chasing dreams on the other hand, that's a different story
Making my dreams into a reality is dope, that kinda feeling is a different glory What is my passion, I asked myself
I had to think hard about because the ideas I was pursuing didn't give me that fire to fuel my motivation, it was just the exact opposite like a ice shelf

But one idea that kept coming back to me was my poetry

I've always been good with words, putting meaningful rhyme schemes together as smooth as butter I guess you can call it flowetry

I am so passionate about my art I had to pursue it

I hesitated long enough, so lemme lace my nikes up and just do it
If a stumbling block gets in my way ima just move it
And No more talking about it, it's time to just show and prove it

"SUCCESS STARTS WHERE?"

Motivation hit me like a brick after I left the networking event

I'm not tryna compete with ya I'm tryna eat with ya, it's enough
paper for all of us to be Lit

Those are the words I heard a young black man around my same
age say well, if it's enough for everybody to eat it's time for me to
go grab a plate
I gotta stay hungry, drinking up every drip of game and eating all
the knowledge like I was at a buffet

but this is real life my family's livelihood depends on my mindset
change because that's where success has to start first, in your mind
because if you don't have the right mindset about what you wanna
do it's not even worth trying

and if you not gonna give it your best effort, when you fail it's not
even worth crying with every success story there's 100 failure
stories
you gotta take risk and bet on ya self because if you don't got no
nuts you definitely won't have no glories

don't broadcast your dreams to everyone especially not ppl who aren't gonna help you make those dreams a reality

everybody ain't rooting for ya, hustle in the dark and let your success shine while it becomes your reality

that's how you start to build generational wealth

passing down generational wealth is great but without the knowledge and wisdom passed down with it the next generation will still need help

so, if you only can remember one thing I said please remember that success starts where?? In your head

"THE LAZY MAN"

A wise man once told me "The Lazy Man works twice as hard"

That's why I work hard now but I still struggle with procrastination
so just to begin is twice as hard

but once I finally start I strive to leave a astonishing remark
i wanna be the best at being me, so me comparing you to me is
something I never wanted to start

I think back on what I've came through and where I am now and I
know it was Jehovah who carried me when I was beat down
beat down by life

ashamed of my situation like a tiger without stripes

but a thinking man is only wise if he learns from the mistakes he
committed

some of my mistakes got me in a jail cell along with a rap sheet
that was no contradiction the lifestyle I was living was foul so being
penalized and punished was a giving
But I aint trippin, I learned a lot during the process, it made me
into the well rounded man I am today

And I strive to work hard not to make those mistakes again because I have to be here to make sure my family is ok

because if I was lazy mentally I might make those same mistakes again and I would have to work twice as hard to right my wrongs again

"THE ANTIDOTE TO FEAR"

Preparation is the antidote to fear

If you are not prepared, fear will win against you every time...
Every second, every minute, every hour, every day, every month,
every year

Do you get the point?

If your fear is taking risk, then you will have to pay the toll in
which fear will take every coin

fear will cause you to procrastinate in getting things done
fear will cause you to not face a problem head on instead fear will
cause you to turn around and run

You may wonder: how will being prepared take away my fears?

when you are prepared you are more confident, when you are
confident you are more decisive and when you are decisive you are
fearless, that's how being prepared takes away your fears

so stand up and stand strong and face your obstacles head on and I promise that you will overcome those challenges every time because you will be prepared to face all your fears until they are all gone

"#AspireToInspire'

Aspire To Inspire is more than a hashtag it's a way of life

It's something I wake up every day to do, so not inspiring someone when I speak to em just doesn't feel right

Aspire To Inspire is more than a hashtag it's what people need

And I'm the voice of the people, and in a world starving people to death with obstacles, INSPIRATION is what I'm cooking up and now it's time to eat

Aspire To Inspire is more than a hashtag I put it in my flesh

I've overcome so much there's no obstacle I can't overcome so when I face new challenges there's no need to over stress

Aspire To Inspire is more than a hashtag it's a daily goal

I can talk to 100 people and if only 1 person feels better after we spoke I would feel better knowing that I achieved that goal

Aspire To Inspire is more than a hashtag It's a legacy

That's why I teach my family to always look for opportunities to
serve others and the joy they receive from seeing others light up
with happiness is sheer ecstasy
Aspire To Inspire is more than a hashtag it's what I stand on

And I Aspire To Inspire others for the rest of my life so folding
under any pressure in the meantime is something I can't do
because I have people relying on me to stay hands on

#AspireToInspire

"THE GRAND ARCHITECT"

Sitting here gazing at the sky as I wonder at Jehovah's creation
From the stars in the night sky to this beautiful earth beneath our
feet is so amazing From every creature moving on the surface of
the ground swimming underwater flying in
the sky

Jehovah God intended this earth to be a paradise and it WILL be
how do I know that you may wonder? Because Jehovah God
CANNOT lie

You see Jehovah is the "Grand Architect" with a great sense of
humor

Look at all the different types of animals, for example mammals
with duck bills, webbed feet and paddle tails called a platypus. Do
you sense the humor?

You see this "Grand Architect" perfectly placed the earth the right
amount of miles away from the sun

A mile closer to the sun we would be burnt alive with nowhere to
run A mile farther we would freeze to death

In either scenario there would not be a plant, human, or animal left See we have a creator for a reason and yes, we need his help We just have to reach out to him and grab his hand, he has already lovingly made the first step

He is Loving, Powerful, Wise, and Just
Jehovah always looks for opportunities to show us his cardinal attributes and to make sure we have a successful happy life, living by Jehovah's wisdom is a must

This is just the beginning (A Day in Paradise)

Today is a very exciting day! I've been waiting for years for this day. Guess what, it is resurrection day! And I was told that this was the day to get prepared to see my Grammy and my mom again. I have been prepping for some time now. Me and my dad built my Grammy a beautiful house that I know she is gonna love. And for my mom, me and my sisters are planning to welcome her back with a live jazz band. She loves jazz so I know she's gonna love it. So now that y'all have the background let us talk about my day. It is 8am, and I did not sleep at all last night due to sheer excitement. Well let's start my day off by getting some perfectly brewed coffee made by my lovely wife, she also made some good breakfast to go with it. We have been in paradise for a few hundred years now and even though we're perfect I still want some bacon for breakfast but it's cool though this paradise fruit is LIT! Afterwards me and Brandy usually go on a walk on the beach in our backyard while just enjoying our time together. We have been married for 300 years so we have a lot of memories to reminisce on. Afterwards we meet up with our kids who are now all grown up, we meet with them so we can discuss one more time how we are gonna welcome back ma and Grammy later on at the resurrection party. Everyone is excited, especially me. I've been longing for this day for a long time, But I still have a few hours to go before the party so I decided to go play with my pet lion. His name is king no pun intended, while I was playing with king my cell phone rings (yes we still have cell phones in paradise) it was my daddy calling, he was also super excited to see my Grammy again. Tonight is gonna be epic! Next I met up with my sisters for lunch. We had a variety of fruits and a huge variety of breads. I didn't know there were that many ways to prepare bread. Anyway, we talked about ma and we were overwhelmed with joy because in a few hours we were gonna see her again. My last memory of seeing my mom alive was distressing. So for me to be able to see her again in full health is gonna be amazing! Well now it is time to meet up with David and Solomon. You probably wonder why huh? Well David is great with instruments and Solomon is great with poetry and we have plans for them to play live music and have some poetry read dedicated to my mom and my Grammy. So we meet up and discuss the plans while having a few beers. Some of my other friends joined us too. We were vibin so good that the time went by pretty fast. Welp we have 1 hour until show time, so I rush home to meet up with Brandy and the kids. We all get dressed up in ball style so you can imagine how dope we look with a perfect mind to have the perfect taste of style. The time is here! David and the band are playing and it sounds great, all my family is there from my kids all the way down to my great great great great grandkids, yep I'm that old but I still have the energy and looks of someone in their 20s. Suddenly the music stops and a loud voice starts speaking from the clouds, no need to guess, it was definitely Jehovah's voice. Next, he calls my mom's name then he calls my Grammy name almost in a sense of an introduction then the band starts back playing. As the music is playing, I see from a distance 2 people walking and dancing to the music as they get closer and I see their beautiful faces. I couldn't hold myself together. The tears of joy started flowing and then both my Grammy and my mama started running towards me and I ran and met them and hugged them. By that time all the other family ran up to meet them as well, everyone had wet eyes but of course it was tears of joy. After everyone spoke we all went and took our seats, I cued Solomon to come up. Once we got on stage David started playing the harp and Solomon started reading a poem he dedicated to my mom and Grammy, it was a beautiful poem which left everyone again with wet eyes. Now let the party begin! We all danced for the whole night. Wheeeww we were all tired so we ended the night. Thank you Jehovah for keeping your promise…

This is just the Beginning!

Made in the USA
Columbia, SC
30 October 2023

25231638R00059